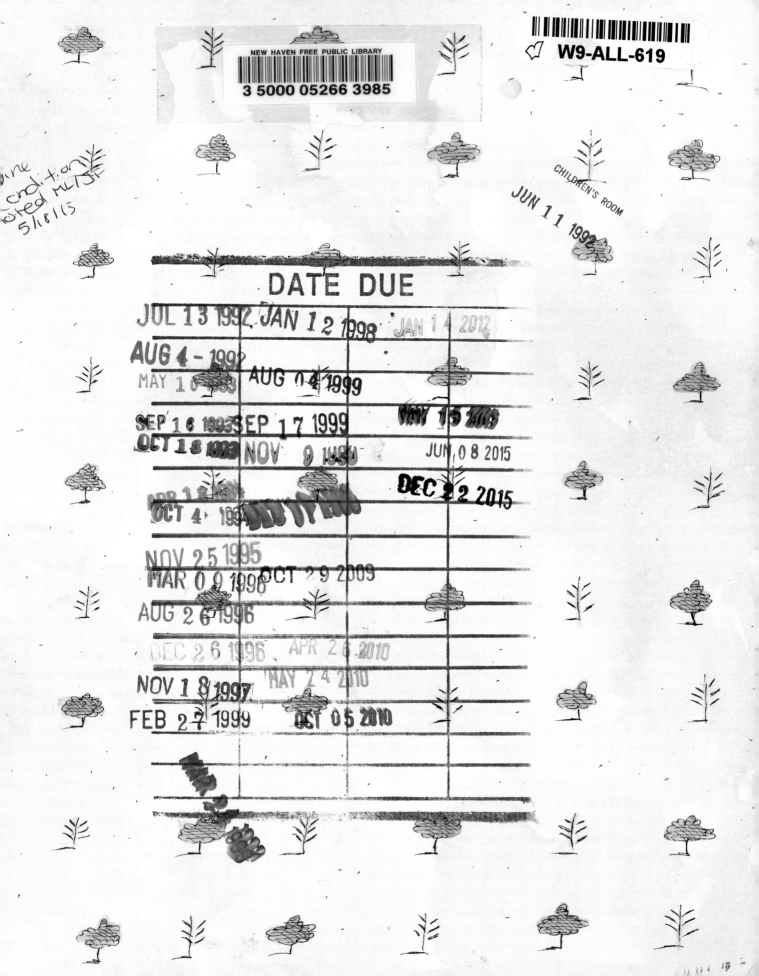

NEW HAVEN FREE PUBLIC LIBRARY

3 5000 05266 3985

W9-ALL-619

CHILDREN'S ROOM

JUN 1 1 1992

fine
condition
noted ML/JF
5/18/15

DATE DUE

JUL 13 1992	JAN 1 2 1998	JAN 1 4 2012
AUG 4 - 1992		
MAY 1 6 1993	AUG 0 4 1999	
SEP 1 6 1993	SEP 1 7 1999	MAY 1 5 2013
OCT 1 8 1993	NOV 8 1999	JUN 0 8 2015
		DEC 2 2 2015
OCT 4 - 1994		
NOV 2 5 1995		
MAR 0 9 1996	OCT 2 9 2009	
AUG 2 6 1996		
DEC 2 6 1996	APR 2 6 2010	
NOV 1 8 1997	MAY 2 4 2010	
FEB 2 7 1999	OCT 0 5 2010	

To my parents

C.V.

Text copyright © 1990 by Margaret Clark
Illustrations copyright © 1990 by Charlotte Voake

All rights reserved. No part of this book may be reproduced in any
form or by any electronic or mechanical means, including
information storage and retrieval systems, without permission in
writing from the publisher, except by a reviewer who may quote
brief passages in a review.

First U.S. Edition 1990
First published in Great Britain in 1990 by Walker Books

ISBN 0-316-14499-1

Library of Congress Catalog Card Number 90-52642
Library of Congress Cataloging-in-Publication information is available.

Joy Street Books are published by Little, Brown and Company (Inc.)

10 9 8 7 6 5 4 3 2 1

Printed in Hong Kong by South China Printing Co. (1988) Ltd.

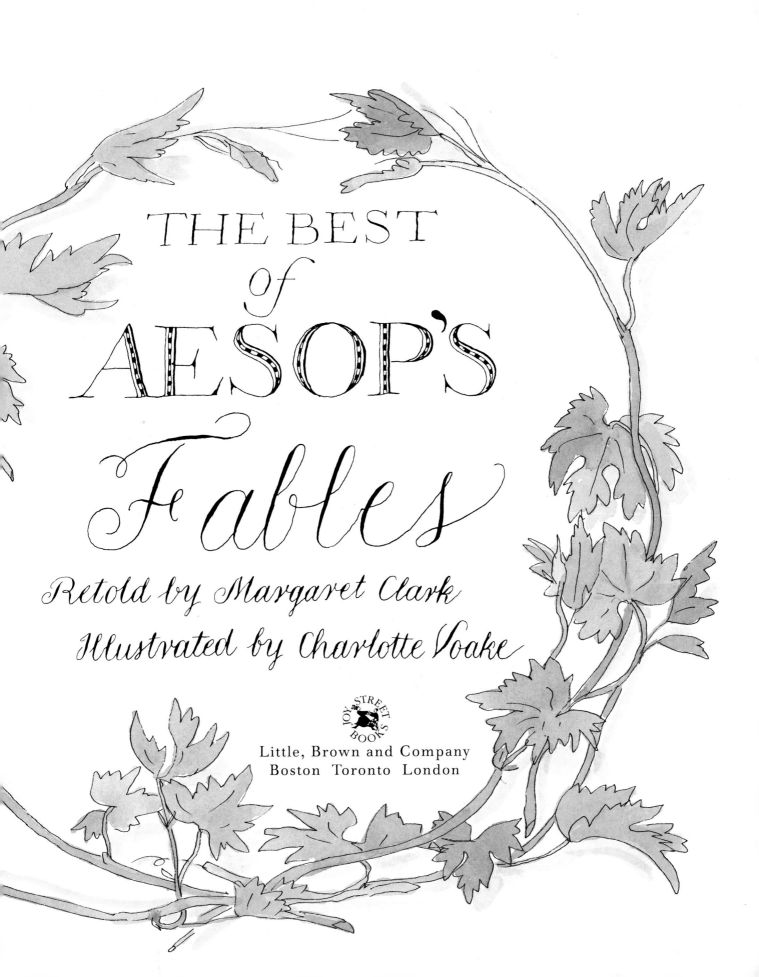

THE BEST
of
AESOP'S
Fables

Retold by Margaret Clark

Illustrated by Charlotte Voake

Little, Brown and Company
Boston Toronto London

Contents

CHILDREN'S ROOM

398.2
C548b

Foreword

I wish I could say that I had loved Aesop's fables as a child, but in my memory they are identified forever with those dauntingly worthy and solid editions of "children's classics" that were chosen by well-meaning adults in the 1930s with intent to teach rather than to entertain. Bound in tooled leather, meant to last a lifetime, they were so intimidating that nothing would have induced me to open books that so plainly declared they were "good for children."

Perhaps that's why the word "fable" has kept the connotation of "do-gooding" for me ever since. That's a shame, for poor Aesop — and no one seems to know exactly who he was — must have told his stories primarily to entertain, to hold the attention of his audience. Almost of secondary importance is the fact that the stories, though peopled by animals, are about human behavior and how, in the end, most of us get our comeuppance if we concentrate too hard on our own concerns and don't think about others in the course of going about our daily life.

If we accept what the scholars tell us, Aesop was what we would now deem "underprivileged," if not handicapped: he was a slave, of legendary ugliness, who lived on the Greek island of Samos in the sixth century BC. The stories ascribed to him were not written down until about 200 years later. So whether he insisted on spelling out the morals underlying his stories we don't know. Charlotte Voake and I decided they were best left unsaid: if children understand and enjoy the stories as we have presented them, they will certainly appreciate the morals behind them. What we have tried to do is to dispel altogether the "preacherly" tone from the best of Aesop's shrewd and funny stories.

Margaret Clark

THE HARE and THE TORTOISE

A hare was one day making fun of a tortoise. "You are a slowpoke," he said. "You couldn't run if you tried."

"Don't you laugh at me," said the tortoise. "I bet that I could beat you in a race."

"Couldn't," replied the hare.

"Could," said the tortoise.

"All right," said the hare. "I'll race you. But I'll win, even with my eyes shut." They asked a passing fox to set them off.

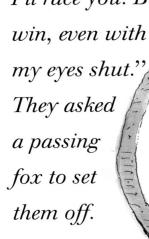

"Ready, set, go!" said the fox.

The hare went off at a great pace. He got so far ahead he decided he might as well stop for a rest. Soon he fell fast asleep. The tortoise came plodding along, never stopping for a moment. When the hare woke up, he ran as fast as he could to the finish line...

9

But he was too late—the tortoise had already won the race!

11

THE FOX and THE CROW

One day a crow snatched a piece of cheese from an open cottage window and flew up into a tree, where she sat on a branch to eat it. A fox, walking by, saw the crow and at once wanted the cheese for himself.

"O Crow," he said, "how beautiful your feathers are! And what bright eyes you have! Your wings shine like polished ebony, and your head sparkles like a glistening jewel. If your voice is as sweet as your looks are fair, you must be the queen of the birds." The unwary crow believed every word, and, to show how sweet her voice was, she opened her mouth to sing. Out dropped the cheese, which the fox instantly gobbled up.

"You may have a voice," he said to the crow as he went on his way, "but whatever happened to your brains?"

THE CAT and THE MICE

A family of mice was being chased every day by a hungry cat.

"What are we going to do?" said Mother, as they all sat around her one evening.

Everyone had something to suggest, but the smallest mouse said, "If we hang a bell around his neck, then we shall hear him coming and we'll have time to get out of his way."

All the mice squealed in excitement and told the smallest mouse how clever he was.

Then the oldest mouse in the family spoke.

"That may sound like a good idea," he said, "but tell me: which one of you is brave enough to go up to the cat and hang a bell around his neck?"

And why do you think none of them answered?

THE FOX and

There was a fox who just loved to make fun of other people. One day he invited a stork to dinner. "I have made some delicious soup specially for you," he said. But when they went to the table, the stork saw that the soup was in a very shallow dish and she could not drink a single drop with her long, pointed bill. The fox laughed when she tried. "So you don't like my soup," he jeered. "All the more for me!" And he lapped the plates clean. The stork was so hurt by the fox's behavior that she made up her mind to get back at him. "Do come to dinner with me," she said. "I know you are fond of soup, so I have made some specially for you."

THE STORK

The fox licked his lips, thinking how stupid the stork was. But when he came up to the stork's table, he saw that she had put the soup in a jug with a long, thin neck and his tongue could never reach it. "Tit for tat," snapped the stork in her prim voice. The fox went home hungry, with his tail between his legs.

THE BOY WHO CRIED WOLF

A boy was sent to look after a flock of sheep as they grazed near a village. It was raining, and he was bored, so he decided to play a trick on the villagers.

"Wolf! Wolf!" he shouted as loud as he could. "There's a wolf attacking your sheep."

Out ran all the villagers, leaving whatever they were doing, to drive away the wolf. When they rushed into the field and found the sheep quite safe, the boy laughed and laughed.

The next day the same thing happened.

19

"Wolf! Wolf!" shouted the boy.
And when the villagers ran into
the field and again found everything
quiet, he laughed more than ever.
On the third day a wolf
really did come.
"Wolf! Wolf!" shouted the boy, as the
sheep ran wildly in all directions.
"Oh, please come quickly!"
But this time the villagers ignored him,
because they thought he was only
playing tricks, as he had done before.
And can you guess what happened next?

THE GRASSHOPPER
and THE ANTS

One winter's day, when the sun came out unexpectedly, all the ants hurried out of their anthill and began to spread out their store of grain to dry.

Up came a grasshopper who said, "I'm so hungry. Please will you give me some of your grain?"

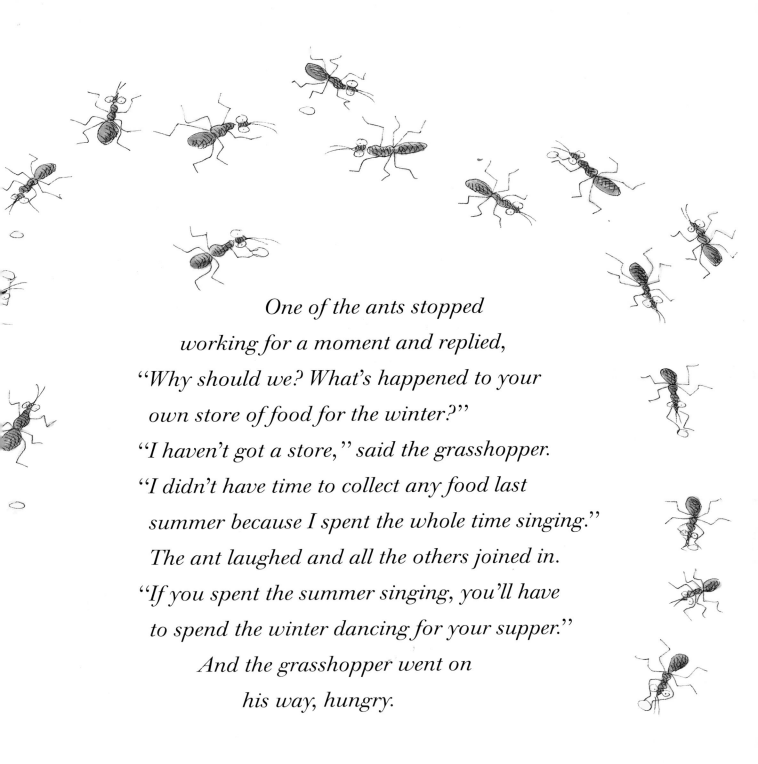

One of the ants stopped
working for a moment and replied,
"Why should we? What's happened to your
own store of food for the winter?"
"I haven't got a store," said the grasshopper.
"I didn't have time to collect any food last
summer because I spent the whole time singing."
The ant laughed and all the others joined in.
"If you spent the summer singing, you'll have
to spend the winter dancing for your supper."
And the grasshopper went on
his way, hungry.

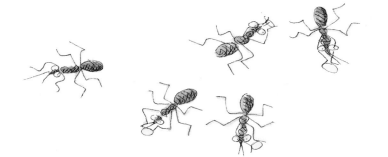

24

THE FARMER'S DAUGHTER

A farmer's daughter was walking home across the fields, carrying a bucket of milk on her head. She was thinking. "Now I have milked the cow, I must churn the milk. When it has turned to butter, I must take the butter to market. When I have sold the butter, I must buy some eggs. When the eggs hatch, I must feed the chickens. When the chickens are fat, I must take them to market. When I have sold the chickens, then I can buy some new clothes." With that, she began to run. But then the bucket fell off her head and all the milk spilled!

THE FOX
and
THE GRAPES

One day a fox, who was hot
and tired and very thirsty,
saw some fat, juicy grapes
hanging from a vine high above
his head. He stood on tiptoe and
stretched as high as he could,
but they were just out of reach.
Then he began to jump, for now he
wanted those grapes more
than anything else in the world.
But the higher he jumped, the
further away they seemed to be.
At last he was so tired he gave up. "I
don't care," he said angrily. "Those
grapes weren't ripe anyway."
(But of course he knew they were...)

THE DOG and THE BONE

A dog was walking over a bridge carrying a large bone in her mouth. Looking down into the stream, she saw another dog there. It was carrying an even bigger bone in its mouth. Immediately, the dog on the bridge jumped into the water, snatching for the bigger bone and dropping her own.

And then there was just one cold, wet dog and no bone at all!

THE FOX and THE GOAT

A fox, who was not looking where he was going, fell down a well and could not get out. While he was wondering what to do, along came a goat.

"What are you doing down there?" said the goat curiously.

"I'm drinking this delicious water," replied the fox.

"Oh, let me have some," said the goat, jumping in too.

The fox let the goat drink until he could drink no more.

Then the goat looked up and said, "Oh, my goodness, how can we get out of here?"

The fox said cunningly, "I have an idea. If you stand on your hind legs and put your front legs against the wall, I can climb up on your back and get out. Then I can pull you up."

"All right," said the goat. But once the fox was out, he laughed and went on his way.

THE BEAR and THE FRIENDS

Two men who were friends were walking along a road together, when out from behind a rock stepped an enormous bear. One of the men leapt up the nearest tree and hung, trembling, from one of its branches. The other man threw himself on the ground and lay very still, pretending to be dead.

The bear sniffed him all over and strolled away. When the bear was out of sight, the man in the tree jumped down. He came over to his friend and asked, "What was that bear doing, whispering in your ear?"

"He was doing me a favor," the man answered. "He told me that if you were a true friend, you'd never have run away and left me here alone."

THE FAT HENS
and
THE THIN HENS

There were a lot of hens who lived together in a farmyard. Some were fat and some were thin and scrawny. The fat hens laughed at the thin ones and called them rude names— "Skinny Lizzie," "Skinny Malinky Longlegs," and "Skinny Banana Toes."

One day the cook was told to prepare a dinner of roast chicken. She went out into the farmyard and all the hens looked up to see which she would choose. Then she picked out all the fat birds, and this time it was the skinny ones who laughed.

THE  LION & THE MOUSE

A lion was dozing in the shade
after a large meal,
when a mouse ran across his tummy.
The lion felt something tickling him, so he put out his paw
and picked up the little mouse, who squealed with terror.
"Oh, please don't eat me," said the mouse. "I'll make such a very
small mouthful. Let me go, and one day
I'll do you a good turn."

The lion laughed. "You! What could you ever do for me?"
But he wasn't hungry so he let the mouse go.

Some weeks later the mouse heard the
lion roaring with pain. The great king
had been caught by hunters and
was tied up with rope.

When the mouse saw this,
he started gnawing at the rope with his sharp little teeth.
It took him a long, long time, but at last the lion was free.
The mouse looked up and said, "There, you see!
You'd be in big trouble if it weren't for me."
Then the lion slunk away
without a word.

35

THE WOLF
and
HIS SHADOW

One day, when the sun was low in the sky, a wolf caught sight of an enormous shadow on the ground beside him. He looked all round, but there was no one else about.

"Why, that's <u>my</u> shadow," said the wolf. "What a wonderful animal I must be! I've never even seen another animal as big as that. The lion calls himself king, but he's not nearly as big as I am. I'm going to be king from now on."

So the wolf strutted about, thinking of all the things he would do now he was king. He was so busy thinking about himself, he didn't even notice the lion, who suddenly sprang on him and swallowed him whole.

As the lion licked his lips, he said, "What a silly wolf! Everyone knows that sometimes your shadow is big, sometimes it's small, and sometimes you have no shadow at all."

THE CRAB
and
HIS MOTHER

"**W**hy can't you walk properly?" complained a mother crab to her baby. "Stop walking sideways."

"I'm only copying what you do," said the little crab. "If you show me how, I'll walk straight."

But the mother crab only knew how to walk sideways, as all crabs do, so what else could the baby do?

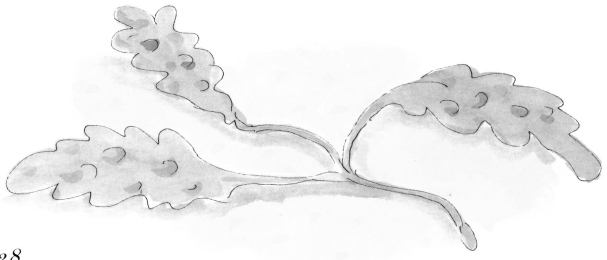

THE NORTH WIND and

The north wind and the sun were having an argument. The north wind claimed to be stronger than the sun, and the sun said, "No, I am the strongest." At last they agreed to have a competition to see who could make a traveler take off his cloak. The wind blew and blew furiously, but the harder it gusted the tighter the man clutched his cloak around him.

THE SUN

Then it was the sun's turn.
At first the sun warmed the
traveler gently with its rays so that
he soon had to unbutton his cloak.
Then the sun shone more and more brightly,
until the man was so hot that he threw
off his cloak and went on his
way without it.

THE TOWN MOUSE
and
THE COUNTRY MOUSE

There was once a country mouse who lived in a field and a town mouse who lived behind the baseboard of a large kitchen. The town mouse went to spend a holiday with the country mouse, and on the first evening they sat down together for a supper of grains of barley and ears of corn.

The town mouse did not like this food at all and said to her friend, "My poor dear, this is no life for you! At my house there are much better things to eat, and if you come and stay you can share them with me."

So they set off at once, without even finishing their meal. When they reached the town, they went into the house, and the town mouse showed the country mouse all around the kitchen, which was filled with cheese and chutney, jam and honey, cake and jelly, and lots of other good things.

The country mouse had never seen anything like it before, and she and her friend were just about to start on this feast when the cook came in through the door. "Quick!" said the town mouse. "Into that hole in the baseboard!"

The country mouse was very frightened and uncomfortable hiding in the hole with her friend.

When all was quiet, the two mice came out again and once more started to eat. Again, the door opened, in came the cook, and again they had to rush for the safety of their hole.

This time the country mouse decided she had had enough. "I'm going home, my friend," she said. "You can keep your cheese, your honey, your cake, and your jelly. I'd rather enjoy my barley and corn in peace, without running into a hole every five minutes!"

46

And off she went…

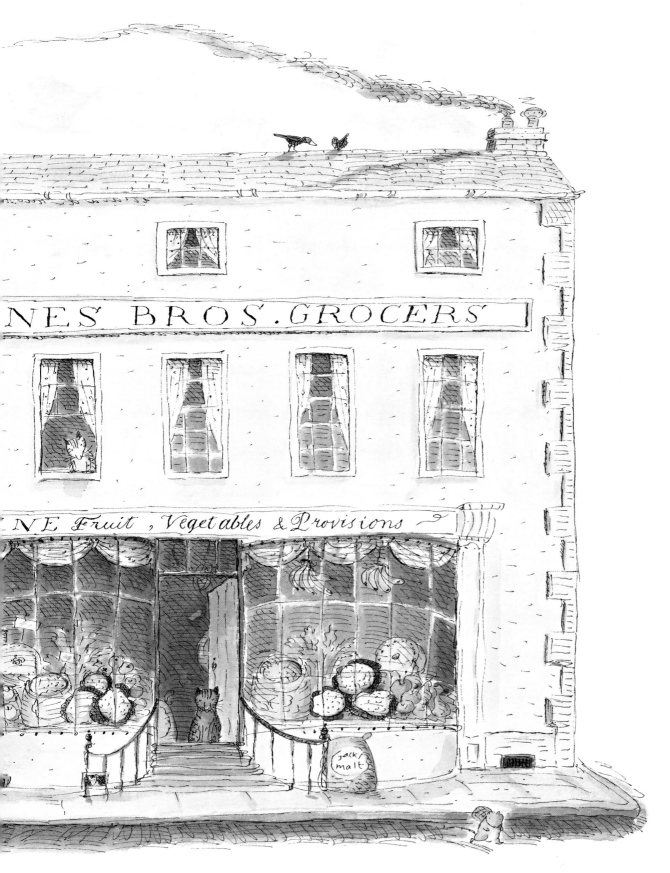

back to her comfortable home in the country.

THE MONKEY
and
THE CAMEL

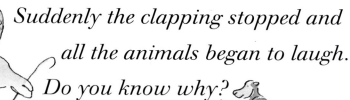

The animals were having a party.
They all sang and danced,
and then the monkey performed the
most astonishing acrobatics.
Everyone clapped and cheered so much that
the camel grew envious of the monkey. So he
decided to try to do some tricks himself and followed
the monkey onto the tightrope.

Suddenly the clapping stopped and
all the animals began to laugh.
Do you know why?

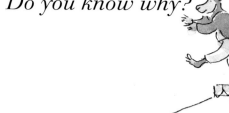

THE LION and THE BULL

A lion had his eye on a fine, fat bull which he thought would make a very good meal.

To persuade the bull to come into his den, the lion said he was roasting a sheep and invited the bull to share it. The bull arrived, looking forward to his supper. But when he came in, he saw that all the pots and pans were empty and the long spit turning over the fire had nothing on it.

"I'm off," said the bull.

"But why?" protested the lion.

"We're not going to eat a sheep," the bull answered. "You're preparing to roast a bull—but you're not roasting me!"

49

THE WOLF and THE HERON

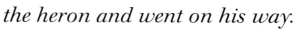

A wolf got a bone stuck in his throat. It hurt so much when he tried to swallow that he went to look for someone who could take it out. Luckily he met a heron and when he saw its long, pointed beak he knew this was just the thing to pick out the bone. So he asked the heron nicely if it would help him. The heron stopped and thought for a minute.

"What will you give me if I put my head in your mouth?"

"There'll be a big reward," gasped the wolf.

The heron put its head inside the wolf's mouth and gently pulled the bone from his throat.

The wolf, now feeling much better, thanked the heron and went on his way.

"Hey!" called the heron.

"What about my reward?"

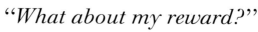

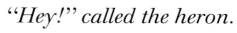

"You've got it," said the wolf. "From now on you can boast
to everyone that you put your head inside a wolf's
mouth and didn't get it bitten off."

THE HEN and THE FOX

A fox went into a henhouse looking for something to eat.
There, high above his head on a perch, sat a large, fat hen.
"My dear girl," he called up to her, "you don't look very
well today. Why don't you come down here so that I can
feel your pulse and take your temperature?"

The hen knew perfectly well what the fox wanted. "I certainly
haven't felt very well since you came in," she said, "but I'm
sure I would feel much worse if you came any closer.
I'm better up here, thank you very much."

THE LION and THE HARE

One day a lion was hunting for his dinner. As he padded
along, suddenly in his path he saw a hare fast asleep. He
stopped, opened his mouth, and was just going to eat her when out
of the corner of his eye he saw a deer running by.
"What luck!" said the lion. "I'd much
rather have deer than hare."

He left the hare asleep and chased
after the deer. But the deer had
a good start and ran faster
than the lion, who soon lost
sight of him altogether.

"Now where did I leave that
hare?" said the lion, furious. But
the hare, who had been woken by the
sound of the lion's paws thudding after
the deer, had long since run away.

"What a nitwit I am," said the lion, who by now was hungry as
well as angry. "Why didn't I eat the hare while I had the chance?"

52

THE ASS and THE WOLF

An ass was quietly grazing in a meadow, when a wolf came into the field. The ass at once began to limp. Up ran the wolf who said, suspiciously, "What's wrong with your foot?"

"I stepped on a thorn," replied the ass. "If you're thinking of eating me, you'd better pull out the thorn first or it will stick in your throat."

"You're right," said the wolf. "Lift up your foot and I'll take a look at it." The ass lifted his foot and the wolf began to examine it. Then the ass let fly with a mighty kick in the wolf's face. "Serves me right," mumbled the wolf through its broken teeth. "My father taught me how to catch and eat animals, not how to heal them."

ZEUS and THE JACKDAW

Zeus, the greatest of the Greek gods, announced that he was going to make one bird king of all the others. He said they must all come to his palace and he would choose the one who was the most beautiful. All the birds went down to the river to wash and preen their feathers, but the jackdaw knew he could never be chosen because his feathers were so dull. Then he noticed that the other birds had dropped some of their bright feathers, so he picked them up and covered himself with them.

When the birds stood before Zeus, the jackdaw looked the finest of them all. "You are the king," said Zeus and called the jackdaw to his throne.

But as soon as the jackdaw moved, all the bright feathers fell off. And he hung his head in shame as he stood in his own drab plumage while all the other birds laughed.

THE DOG in the MANGER

One day a greedy dog went into a horse's stable and jumped up into the manger, which was full of barley. When the dog tasted the barley, he didn't like it at all and spat it out.

Along came the horse, all ready for his supper, but the dog snapped and growled and wouldn't let the horse anywhere near the barley.

"But you don't want it," said the horse.

"No, but I'm not going to let anybody else have it either," said the dog.

THE MILLER,
HIS SON,
and THEIR DONKEY

A miller was driving his donkey to market. His young son trudged along behind him. "How silly you are!" said a girl they passed on the road. "Why make your son walk when he could ride on the donkey?" "What a good idea!" said the miller, and he lifted his son on to the donkey's back. The miller went on driving the donkey but soon he began to feel very hot.

"How silly you are!" said a friend of the miller's who came up behind them. "You spoil that son of yours. Why don't <u>you</u> ride the donkey and make him walk?"

"What a good idea!" said the miller, lifting the boy off the donkey's back and mounting it himself. The boy soon began to trail far behind.

"How selfish you are!" said a woman sitting by the roadside. "Why don't you let the boy ride with you?"

"What a good idea!" said the miller, lifting the boy up beside him.

After a while the donkey was so tired it could hardly put one foot in front of the other.

"How silly you are!" said a traveler, passing them. "If you ride that donkey all the way to market, it will be worn out when you get there, and no one will buy it. You'd better carry it and give it a rest."

"What a good idea!" said the miller. He got off the
donkey and lifted his son down. Then they tied
the donkey's legs together and carried it upside
down on a pole. The donkey was very frightened.
It kicked and struggled so much that, just
as they were passing over a bridge,
its ropes broke and it fell
into the river. And they
never saw it again.

THE WOLF and THE SHEPHERD

There was once a wolf who had tried again and again to steal a sheep, but the shepherd guarded his flock so carefully that he drove the wolf away every time he appeared. One day the wolf had an idea. He took a fleece that had been sheared from one of the sheep, put it on his back, and then strolled into the meadow.

Neither the shepherd nor the sheep recognized him. The wolf headed straight for the fattest of the sheep and opened his jaws to seize it by the throat, when suddenly he heard the shepherd behind him. "Now which of them is fat enough for me to eat?" said the shepherd. Then the shepherd picked up the wolf—and carried him off to the kitchen for his supper!

MAY 5 1992